The Only Universe I have Ever Known

Taiyu John Robertson

ISBN 978-0-6151-7296-5

TABLE OF CONTENTS

Miami

Miami was wicked hot
and even though we landed at midnight
I got sweaty
just being outside
wading through
that soupy wall of humid goo
to smoke the first cigarette
I'd had
in hours.

We got a room
up high in some beach hotel,
and sat out until five,
drinking on the balcony.

The sunrise
broiled us out of bed
around 6.

I got real drunk
every night,
just like home,
though the change of scenery
somehow made it different,
and kinda better.

Lulu worried
I'd go over the rail
but I wasn't afraid,
just stupid.

My boy thought the pool was cool,
and the monkeys and dolphins too,
though he got tired
of us driving around
so much
because stuff was always so far away.

It was a weird vacation
what with the kid stuff
all day
and the drinking
all night.

Life was like that all the time
by then,

getting blind drunk
and passing out
then faking my way
through the next day,
every day.

The ocean was nice, though,
and so were the monkeys.

the path

there's no recipe
for living life
with an open heart

you just have to go forward
without thinking or planning
or measuring and mixing

because there ain't no cookbooks
for what to do
here and now

and although
you may not want to hear it
truth isn't necessarily
magical sweet buttery goodness either

not always
ands maybe not ever

so if what you seek
is a snug cocoon
of warm covers and cookies
then this's not for you

and no one ought be blamed
for turning elsewhere
from the rocky mapless path
they cannot help
but walk

An Angry Guttural Roar

Every afternoon when I was a kid
my mother would take a nap.

It didn't matter
what the rest of us did
during that time,
so long as we let her sleep.

I was too young to know that
though, and assumed
the rule still was
that I had to ask first
before going somewhere
or doing something out of the ordinary.

It only took
one screaming raging blow
to the back of my head, however,
to realize how wrong I was.

I can still hear
that angry guttural roar,
and see her fly up from the bed at me
swinging her fists.

And I can still feel
what I felt then,
as I ran out of the house,
screaming and crying,

still uncertain
if it was right or not
to go across the street
to the polo fields,
and what made me
such a bad little boy.

I never again
woke her up
from anything,
no matter what,

and learned real fast
the importance
of not causing waves
or trying to make my mother
do anything
she didn't want
to have to do.

The Last Run

He's already fearless,
careening down the snowy hill
over and over,
hitting the jumps
gaining air
flying

until the Sun's gone
and the wind drives even the bravest
indoors

where with red cheeks and burning ears
he strips off the wet layers
and collapses exhausted
in the knowing
how wonderful
everything truly is,

all of which
takes me back
to my own time
on steel running sleds
and steep icy hills,
where we'd go for hours
not caring
about the cold
or the wind

on the big hill
where Nick's dad died
not long after
his other son's body
came back from Vietnam.

That's how this ends,
you know,

when you can't blot out
the knock
at the door
or the blood on the green
any longer.

By Spring
Nick was in jail
and headed for more trouble,

Danny went away to his Dad's
and came back with one eye gone
from an industrial accident,

and Tommy and I had our stomachs pumped
and got put on probation
until around the time high school ended.

But that last Winter
every day
we sailed blind high fast
and stupid fearless,

down cliffs of ice
and out onto the frozen pond
at the bottom

where the runners let go
and sent us spinning
into joyful
frozen piles
of laughing fading innocence.

My son's got a few years left
before he starts noticing the cold
and maybe a few more
before snow's just something to dread,
like how so many of us end up seeing it eventually.

So sipping coffee
I watch him fly
from the top
over and over,
laughing and screaming
when he hits the jump just right
and gains good air,
as the sled goes one way
and arms and legs another.

Breathing hot steam
from the cup
my teeth chattering
belly shivering
these memories caterwauling,

the sunset finally turns everything
a near single silver tone
and I think how nice
inside will be

before letting him talk me into
just one more run,
yet again

Atone

Every morning when I get up,
and before teeth brushing or face washing
I recite the Gatha of Atonement.

It reminds me
of my own beginningless karma,
born of body speech and thought.

It reminds me
of what I've done,
the thoughts I've had,
the words I've spoken.

It reminds me
of all those
whose karma comes,
at least in part from me.

It reminds me
of the gifts
of those who came before,

whose own thoughts
words and deeds,
now today
leave me
lighting incense,
and reciting prayers
before I brush my teeth.

For you
whose suffering
I have not alleviated,

for you,
whose suffering
gave birth to mine,

I now make full
and open
confession.

Cagefight

The first call came before breakfast
about a woman throwing the guy's barbeque grill
off the balcony
right before the cops got there.

The second was from someone in jail,
wanting to plead guilty,
then not guilty,
then guilty again.
He called back three times in five minutes.

At nine o'clock pretrials
the fellow with the harassment charges
didn't much like
me being insufficiently sympathetic
to how it was
the other guy
ending up in the cagefight
with the Indian
somehow proved how innocent
he really was.

Later the phone rang again;
it was my recovery friend
upset about being in the hospital,
with enough alcohol in her body
to kill 90 percent of all other human beings,
because they won't let her smoke.

Then the forger with AIDS showed up
all the way from Chicago,
where he probably has
about six months or less to live,
just wanting
no matter what
not to die
in prison.

By the end of the day,
if I was still
a drinking man,
I'd be about ready
to get shit faced.

That's not me anymore.
At least not all I am;
and this stuff
doesn't exact the price
it did before,
where there's only so much
to go around,
and after that
I'm an empty hole.

You can go through your life
like that if you want,
where what happens
is always
either good or bad,
right or wrong,
fair or not.

Where your giving
remains contingent
on some sort of salvation
or approval

or even just
the ego boost
that comes
from doing good deeds.

I've had my fill of such ways, though,
and seek
to seek nothing
but the next right thing
for its own sake
before the sun sets and the day ends
and these tired but not so weary bones
settle into the sleep
that comes
to those
seeking peace.

No Worse nor Better

What I wanted to say
was that these moments of clarity,

where you find yourself realizing
formerly hidden truths,
never end,

nor come fully assembled
or pre supplied
with detailed plans,

and no matter how vociferous
or sanctimonious
the claims made,
books written,
or stories told,

there ain't no
ready made recipe
for truth and happiness
laying out there
in some program
or faith
or creed
or club.

But such a speech,
must so far
flow from anger,

and I have pretty much
finally learned
spewing out
the fire my head cooks up
isn't particularly helpful
to anyone but me

and probably not even that.

So I sat back
and played solitaire,
listening
and letting go,
after a fashion;

when my turn came,
I passed,

none the worse

than when I got there,
an hour earlier.

Maybe even
a little better.

Where the Universe Makes Its Home

You go out every day
and find your own truth,
bringing it in from the cold,
tasting its flavor,
seeing what fits and what doesn't,

thinking all along,
how what got you
this far,
way back when
doesn't quite reach
where it needs to go
now.

And still, if you really need to,
you can beat yourself up
and show how wrong you were,
repenting the old ways
ripping shirts and robes,
before getting on
with whatever truth
the truth is now,

but such antics
aren't demanded
by anyone
who matters
or by anything
that counts.

Its the truly courageous ones
who see this clearly,
you understand,

and thereby come
to finally know
the reality
that breathes
and cries
and grows
and changes

in the mind
of true self
that flows
where the universe
makes its home.

memoir

i would write a memoir
from the places where i stood
all along the line

the surly teen
hippie
social worker
biker
philosopher
lawyer
husband
father
drunk
buddhist

and give skin and voice and color
to these aching bones
parched lips
and wrinkled eyes

from which
some sort of truth
might indeed
glean and grace
the spinning sky

Life and Death

If you were told
you're already dead,
as inevitable as the next breath
follows the last,
what would you do?

There's reason enough in this,
for why we drink,
and sleep,
and fuck,
and smoke and eat and love,

not to mention build
and attack,
and possess,
and destroy,

because such endeavors
stem the inexorable tide
of what we fear
will be
a bitter dark conclusion.

The small cuts
and bruised fruit
of ended innocence
lost love
racing time

conspiratorial
markers
for how this ends,
already.

So,
what now?

Easy

There are pills
in my bathroom cupboard
which if taken
in sufficient quantity
will kill anything.

My doctor gave them to me
a few years ago
when I was depressed
and thinking the worst.

They're a loaded gun,
you understand,
in a fancy foil package.

I didn't kill myself,
mainly because the thought
of leaving that gift
to my son
to let go of
the rest of his life
was something
even I wasn't selfish enough
to pull off,

though I sure do understand
why others
don't have
such reservations.

The Itch and the Need to Scratch

Sometimes the tiniest things
make the biggest difference.

Like when I figured out
the space between the itch
and the scratch.

Such a foolish realization
works pretty good
for sleeping feet, too.

So when out of the blue
it got so dark
not even shadows
ventured out,

and I curled up
under the blankets
and pretended to watch crap
on television
while the dishes
and cigarette butts piled up

it was remembering
that gap
that finally
got me up
and going
again.

The Doom

It creeps up on you
slow, subtle,
unseen

a familiar sense of dread
always present,
felt, unfelt,

even in the good times
you just know
won't last,

and of course,
the bad,

crowding out
green Spring days
and languid Summer nights
so much so that eventually
the good stuff
never really comes
at all
anymore.

That's how this one's demons
appear,
and when the monkey's roar
is loud enough,
its all you can do
to keep from screaming.

I was going on thirty
before it dawned on me
not everyone carries such luggage.

Then I'd briefly wonder
what there is
that makes
me like this,

though such questions
inevitably drown
in the pudding like fear
of how far down
it'll go
before the next bounce.

Old Friends

I run into old friends
here and there
from the rum and coke days

they seem embarrassed
like something bad happened
or maybe worried
I'll get evangelical
with the whole sobriety Buddhist kick
its said I'm on

there's usually a bit
of uncomfortable chit chat
about what's new and the weather

but you can tell
they just hope
I'll go away

that's ok
though what I want to say
about how much I miss those times
and wish there was a way
to still do some of it
without destroying everything
in the process
doesn't get a chance
to come through

which is not to say
I'm all high and mighty
about being a sober drunk,
like its something special

I know people
who see it that way

just goes to show
you can puff up your ego
with damn near anything

nor is it bad
not to be able
to run with the big dogs

it just is

same as how
it just is
to bang into these folks
at Walmart
and watch how they fidget
and flop around
until I shake hands
and run along
before things get
worse for them
then they already are

its

its the step off the top
of the 100 foot pole
and the corner where you cannot
move an inch;

its home after jail
collapsed on the hallway floor weeping,
and the place where there's absolutely
no known clue
what to do next;

its the blind in the dark
and the roaring staggering sea;

its the atomic realization
the world will not be conquered
and there ain't enough smokes and sex
to get through just this night,
much less the rest of your life,

and its getting old and
knowing how death might really feel,
and not caring

that gets you to the point
where maybe
for the first time ever
there's a chance
this present moment
might actually be

the one you finally

solely

purely

notice

before being bounced back out

into the cold

wet place

you always thought before

was all there really was.

Ain't Two in the First Place

Brittle squeaky ice
covers everything
and makes the cars run bad
and fingers not work

though the sun stays out
a bit longer
and we're past
Valentines
heading for Presidents

so that the time
when this frozen business
starts getting really really old
is likely to kick in
any day now

I'm not complaining
sitting here as it is
drinking hot coffee
in a leather chair
with pretty paintings
and smart music

There's an old woman
in a long brown cloth coat
pulling a suitcase like wheelie thing
and walking by
with her own coffee

She's not outside much
you can tell
because though wrapped up pretty good
its ultimately only enough
to get from the car to the store
and not much farther

Not like the guys by the library
those bastards are bundled tight
with every layer they got
so only breathing parts
and eyes poke out
as they make their way
wherever

You won't see them in this place
where there's 5 flavors of joe
and a three station cappuccino machine
for the latte crowd

You won't see
suitcase woman
sharing a couple of 40s
with them either

which makes it all even
if it weren't for the fact
this is not a competition
and their world and her world
ain't two
in the first place

Ice Storm

But the storm makes everything beautiful,
though not without a price
as the loose karma
of what winter brings
these fallow fields and cozy homes
means some face struggle
while others
get merely a cheery fire
and frosty windows.

None of that
defeats
the icy hush
of sharp frozen stillness
blanketing these streets and yards.

Nor is it anything special;
just the way,
sometimes warm and bright,
sometimes cold and dark,
here with snow and ice,
there with a quick Spring rain.

They say its not the storm blowing,
anyhow,
just the work of mind.

I say the ice

coating and polishing the world

to an apparent stop

is no less

nor more

than two days before,

so warm then

the robins believed

it was time to build nests.

Dance

I am at a dance
in a dance
dancing

no one else knows
what this is
usually I don't either
though today clarity rears
an ugly head
in place of old fog and cotton

Elaborate rituals
built on sticks
jutting from mud
make waltzing seem
real desperate important
even if when the camera cuts away
worker bees scurry to pull down the world
rearrange the lights for the next number

Watching my feet
I slide into role
here now's the move
the image the idea
popping into view
where instead of this
its us all together

breathing for breath

eating to eat

loving in love

dancing

just

to dance

Being

When someone asked me yesterday
how I was doing,
I glanced up
to see his face
and saw the question
wasn't meant
as a mere pleasantry,

it dawned on me
that I didn't really know what to say
because I hadn't thought too much
on the status of being
for awhile.

Stopping for a second
and turning,
I said I guess I'm doing OK,
now that I think about it,

before walking along
on the way
to whatever else
comes up next
in life.

Perfect Sleep

I was a hibernating bear
changing positions in winter's cave
because my foot fell asleep
or bones started aching.

Wandering blindly,
chattering to no good end,
utterly convinced
the next best thing
was the it
I sought.

All the while
wearing down,
rubbed raw,
frantic to grasp
some cozy warm place
where suffering ends
and struggle ceases.

It wasn't until
almost fifty years passed
that any of this
began to clear up.

The timing
was just about
perfect.

Springfield, Illinois

My parents built a house in Springfield, Illinois
on a dead end next to a cornfield,
back when Johnson was President.

My oldest sister was married,
the middle one away in college in Missouri,
and me in a room in the basement
with red carpeting and paneled walls.

We were supposed to live there forever
and never move again.

I learned to smoke cigarettes
and kiss girls in that town.
We rode bikes, played touch football,
hung out at the Fina station,
listened to the Beatles,
grew our hair long
and wished we could have gone
to Woodstock.

In that town,
as children always finally do,
I put my toys away forever.

They killed Kennedy and King
on TV there;
walked on the moon,
gave me Fear and Loathing in Las Vegas,
and a pawn shop electric guitar.

We moved again, of course;
out of state that next Summer.
I should have known
all along.

After that,
nothing was ever the same.

A few years back
I rode through on my own,
and saw how most everything had changed.

The house was still there,
though not on a dead end anymore;
the cornfield was gone and I can't imagine
they still had the same paneling
in the basement.

There weren't any kids on Stingrays
swooping along the streets either,
but the closed Fina station
looked pretty much
like always.

I got a room
out by the highway,
and fell asleep knowing
no one not already under the covers
was ever coming home
again.

With Love

Sometimes the next right thing
looks pretty damn obvious,
if for no other reason than because
there's always laundry to fold
or dishes to wash
or rugs to vacuum
or letters to write
or papers to file
or zazen to sit.

Other times
the work's more subtle,
misty,
opaque,

like what to do
with love.

Cities of Gods

Somewhere along the endless queue
stretching back
through murky time,

it occurred
to we poor fools,
we sentient ones,
we allegedly
conscious beings,

the idea
that in knowing truth,
redemption comes

and then in turn,
we were to be
the thing -
the truth -
we sought.

A vast and shining city,
this insight slowly built
on right and solid ground,
ascending upwards,
endless, pure,
reaching out
for glorious heaven.

To be like Gods,

to fly and sing,

beyond the end of days,

we sought

in cold and blindness

to pierce the veiled fogged mist.

And so on dreams

were made great cages

of finest hangman's rope,

but gone unseen

where fool's endeavors

led us all along.

Like clouds,

walls vanish

cities die,

and dreams of heaven

fade,

though lighted candles

left behind

still pierce the blind

night's air.

Every Moment Of It

I got high
in school
every day
from 10th grade on,

and even if ambivalent now,
have to say
I loved nearly every moment of it.

I also took enough acid then
to reach the point
where watching the walls breath
and your face melt
got boring.

The pot quit working too,
so that pretty much
half way through college,
the happy funny hungry horny buzz
got replaced
with pointless
nervous worry,

so that when I finally landed
out in the world
my drug days were done,
but not the urge
to find a way
to taste and feel
nirvana.

The Lion's Roar

Amidst these ruined
lost small minds
and tiny ego selves,
the choice appears
to crave and weep
and grasp at summer clouds,

of true despair,
a hell best left unspoken,
of glorious heights
where sensuous passion
sates starved bony shelled beasts
lying pretty, lazy, caged
and struck down dumb
until such time
as death comes round.

Or turning inward,
through and on,
to mountain's summit,
ocean's floor,

the moon
the sun
the wind at rest

the lion's roar.

When the Still Thought Fades

When the still thought fades
so all that's left
rattling around
up here in the attic
is straight back
breathing
at the wall,

then the moment
stretching out
swallowing up
making nice,
shows its true colors
and warm scent

for the whole universe
in the cup
of gently laid hands.

Shuffle

There I was
trying to plead out my guy
after more than a year
of him screwing around
and the prosecutors screwing around
and probably even a little bit
of me screwing around.

He's already serving
a quarter century in prison
for something pretty bad from before,
and this new charge gives him
another 25
lined up
front to back,

so there was every reason
to trade a plea
for a deuce
plus no minimum
to go.

Thing is, though,
its not easy admitting sex
in prison at all,

much less the kind where your new lover
isn't so happy
about that turn of events.

Its not the punk that makes it hard,
but being
a rapist and a fag
in exactly the worst possible place
for such a state of affairs.

So when we finally got
to the moment of truth,
where you either do the deal
or go to trial and lose,
even then it took a bit of work
to make what needed to happen happen.

Which is why,
after that
when the State tried to balk
on their own damn offer,

I about came unglued.

***

There's a certain kind of insanity
that comes to those whose job it is
putting people in prison;

It sucks the blood from their heart,
woefully undernourished already,
leaving only bitterness
and bile
where the compassion's
supposed to go.

But I'm biased,

having spent a very long time

holding hands

with the same folks

they revile,

and judge,

and lock away

or try to kill.

I know their smell

and taste

and texture

and thoughts.

I been to their homes

and ate their food,

listened to their stories,

cried with their children.

And I know

they ain't no different

than you

or me.

So now that we've gotten

to the part,

when you jump out of your chair

in arrogant contemptuous indignation

as to how a good person

would never

do this or that

or any such awful thing

well, I just nod my head
and recollect
how its only the lucky and the stupid
who don't know
what true
unvarnished
desperation
does to the souls
of mere mortals.

***

Sometimes I get where
the complaining
by my clients
merges with the complaining
of the State,
so that you can't tell
when one voice ends and the other starts,

proving yet again
how hurting others
never makes you
not a victim.

And while its usually
water off the duck and all,
this time there's something heavy
in the way it goes down,

until I remember,

no matter how good or bad a deal it was,

the guy in orange

ultimately invariably shows

a certain grace,

leaving the courtroom,

legs chained,

down the elevator,

out to the van,

off to hell again,

while the prosecutors wallow

in smugness,

ranting and raving

about justice done,

and though always arrogant,

never ever

letting go

of the few times

they don't get their way

with the entitled exacted retribution

they just knew

was due.

In the end when the smoke cleared
it all went through easy enough,
and I headed back to the office,
the prosecutor went back
to tell her colleagues
how awful I am and the rapist was
and judges are,
and everything,

and my guy
very quietly
went back to prison
to finish
his 27 year
sentence.

A Just and Loving Lord

Its easy to narrow yourself down
to simple measures
of pretty and ugly,

and then assign
all the people
and all the things
in all the worlds
into one of them two boxes.

Its an elegant scheme
for making sense
and providing direction
so you don't have to feel
much more
than your own appalled indignation
at the stuff
in the bad boxes,

though someday
according to the plan
it'll all be gone
locked away
or dead,

and the trumpets of heaven
will finally play
in the perfect fields
of a just
and loving lord.

Universe

At Ryumonji when you go outside on a clear night
there are millions of stars doming the cereal bowl sky,

so bright as to seemingly light up
the trees and fields
in an eerie silver glow.

I'll stand there,
away from the porch
in the dark
smoking and looking up,

amazed and humbled
at the contrast
between self centered foolishness
and the true size
of the universe,

before putting out
my cigarette
and getting inside
to sleep
before 5:00 zazen.

Kingdom

It was the lucky ones
who got to 18
before the babies and the shitty jobs
kicked in.

Even then,
between the divorces,
and the crank,
and the layoffs,
and everything else that happens,
you never know
who'll make it
someplace
where there's time
to dream
even a little
about having a life worth living
once in awhile,

in the kingdom of strip malls
and pink eye,
where the kids run wild in the front yard
and the elders drink vodka and beer
out back,

where the incessant braying
of local television
makes you think nirvana
comes with a side of baby back ribs
and a Big Gulp,

and even though
we're just a fungus
infesting a tiny little planet
in just one
of a hundred million galaxies
splaying out
across the universe,

everyone still talks
about God
who made us,
looks like us,
thinks like us,
and killed his kid
for us

so that one day soon
we can go to heaven
and live forever
in a kind of peace
and harmony
most of us
have never
ever
taken the time
to imagine,

don't believe we deserve,

and wouldn't know what to do with,
if it happened.

Inch or Two

Waking up
never stopped

I just quit noticing
anything
farther than
an inch or two
from my face

Holiday Inn

We didn't vacation much.
Maybe two or three times, ever,
and then always
just a trip
to see old relatives
in worn out towns
before they died.

The best part
was the driving itself,
and staying in
Holiday Inns
built like square horseshoes
around a pool.

I loved the ice machines
and the color TVs
and how cool it was
sleeping in those air conditioned
way clean
big bed rooms,

eating hamburgers
and french fries,
for breakfast,
plain.

Driving through cities and towns,
where me and my father
someday wished we'd live,
and my mother just wanting
to get wherever it was
we were going.

I understand now
how frightening
all this was
to her.

Some people
hear the lure of the open road
as music;

others,
not so much.

Believe

At some point
its probably a pretty good idea
to figure out
what you believe

and then decide
whether you ought to believe
it any more.

I've done that
a time or two
in life.

Its like
rearranging the living room furniture;
kinda makes things feel new again,

at less
than half
the price.

Dogstars and the Sea

The idea
of ultimate purpose
is surely
merely
neurotic conceit

left over
from when
what we didn't know
far exceeded
what we needed
to survive

and even then
that effort
seemed far far
to much
merely for its own mundane sake

plus we got
these big
squishy
throbbing thingys
up top
spewing
and figuring
and comprehending

so its no surprise
the spaces between
here and there
and the distance
thereafter
got filled

with how special
and godlike
and front row
we just have to be.

     Every dog I've ever had
     would lay there
     fast asleep

     and often as not
     while doing so woof
     and move its paws
     and whimper
     sometimes even bark

     dreaming its own

     heroic tale
     of dogstars
     and wolves

     while the water
     in the tiny little creek
     outside my son's mom's house
     probably not fantasizing at all

continues its inexorable
victory march
to the greatness
of the sea itself.

The tendency
to arrogance
mine and your
notions entail
seems to run
from the taproot

informing even
the smallest cell
in the tiniest bone
of the littlest toe

so that
the innocuous
suggestion
that these
are all just
foolish ideas
gives most people
the willies

such that
like dogs
we whimper and move our paws
build pyramids
shoot rockets

to the end

that heaven

eternity

immortality

meaning itself

finally rears its glorious head

and we shall then

come to know

our march to the sea

has ended

I Knew the Look

she said maybe
and seemed pretty happy
about reaching out

with me
already more than halfway
in her direction

we laughed and closed the gap
finally after so long

talked about the house
and the child
and the future

and when she said
she couldn't imagine
life without me
I floated
about an inch
above the floor

but there's
whatever it was
and there's whatever
this is

and the two don't meet up so good
in the middle

so when the subject
of that other person
rose up

and I saw how her face lit
when I told her she called

and felt the surge
when she dashed out
for coffee and chat
after all these months

I didn't need
any more clues

I knew the look
because I saw it before
back when it was me
she thought about

so that's why
I'm sitting here
now
with this still open heart
leaking blood
all over the fucking floor
again

Coffee Shop

I sit in this one coffee shop
after work sometimes
sharing the space
with a hoard
of college students.

They live in their heads
and in their hearts,
with all the eager zealous frenzy
of kittens learning to hunt mice,

getting down on all fours,
whiskers twitching
eyes zeroed in,

never realizing
their tail sticking out
and jigging here and there
probably dooms
the kill.

It doesn't matter
because at that age
there's nearly no room
for humility

nor dignity,
which when you think about it
isn't such a bad thing.

Running From Ghosts

I found somewhere
back down the line
a sense of doom
lived deep within

lurking
just below
or above
the fog line
of awareness.

Its a subtle haunting,
a foreboding fear,
where you just know
beyond all doubt,

whatever you think
you need
you'll never get
can't keep
and don't deserve

where the best there is
has a two drink minimum,
and takes your wallet and keys
while you're passed out
on the bathroom floor.

I thought I could tame
this insipid despair
with pot and acid,
sex and love,
work and money,
rum, Irish whiskey,
and gin martinis,

all of which
did their part
well enough,
I suppose,

though even fools
like me
can't confuse
oblivion with nirvana
forever.

So, not counting cigarettes and coffee,
I gave it all up,
electing instead
to see what happens

when you stop running
from ghosts and pain.

Its funny, now
looking back a ways
into the gloom and shadowed past,
how at the time everything seemed
so bad,

like concrete and granite,
as real as these tables and chairs
and trees and sky.

Maybe even more.

The Buddha taught
that with our thoughts
we make the world.

Grasping this,
pain flies,
like eagles
trolling northward in Spring
searching elsewhere
for their fish.

My Fingers Got Soft

Got my first guitar from a pawn shop
in the 6th grade
learned to play Gloria
Wild Thing
a few lead riffs

Joined a band in high school
no one was brave enough
to sing
Still had enough going
to think someday
we'd be rock stars

But Nick was the only one
who kept at it
no surprise there
music flowed out of
anything he touched

I kept playing
for 35 more years

It was therapy

But my fingers got soft and bled
forgot where the notes go
not like before

Music's a young man's thing
always will be
but you keep the axe
and flat top

Just in case
just in case

Corner

I don't like throwing stuff away
because memory's
the closest thing
I got
to roots.

And these things
bring it all roaring back

They're in boxes

set in rows
down in the basement
going all the way back
into the dark
where the lightbulb's
gone
in the corner.

Black Wind

The black wind whistled cold and sharp
across my skin tonight in the dark
as we traveled
me and the bike
across town
for breakfast
coffee
with four others like me
who wrap their identity tight
and thick
around the past and its current obsession
over eggs, double bacon
and talk
of psilocybin,
infidelity
and a friend's daughter
turned 18 living
with the old man
up in North Liberty.

The pie was good too.

So Instead I Sit

My teacher told me
a long time ago
if all I'm doing
sitting
is daydreaming
then I may as well
go play golf
or something
for all the good it does.

So instead I try
to just sit
with my back straight
and legs crossed
eyes open, slightly down
not focused
on anything
nor nothing

breathing
unrestrained
a clear bright surface
purely reflecting
the open sky

until
the time
to rise.

The Whatever Thing

One minute
you're blindly stumbling
through what was always
taken
for granted
as real life,

the next minute
its all different
changed
new,

like being awakened
from some kind of
marathon dreamsleep,

so at first
nothing's right
there's no more autopilot

and the rules
look different,
maybe even gone.

I've had a few of these.

You, too.

They're common;
happen all the time.

Like in the face
of illness,
a birth,
or death.

Always in death.

Where suddenly
you realize
how wonderful
or awful
or graced
or unfair
life is.

The trigger
doesn't matter;
whatever it is
those things
you think
are only as real
as thinking
has to be.

And re, the truth,
well that's far bigger
than any
mere
thought
could ever
comprehend.

The problem though,
is that most of us
most all of the time
instead of knowing
who we are
what our lives are
and how it is
really being awake
in the universe,

we just do
whatever it takes
to get through
the whatever thing
that woke
us up in the first place,

in order
to get
back to sleep
as fast
as possible.

So we think,
organize,
make concepts,
build theories,
invent conspiracies,
re-arrange
the mental fluff
inside the bone and skin
we call our heads,

until something
clicks
like clockwork
tics
like a stop watch
and hums
like a turbine.

Its not a bad thing
making up stories
and then confusing
that with the real.

I do it
all the time,

like right now.

But just for a second
imagine the glimpse
that comes
when you open your eyes
for perhaps only an instant

and wonder what it'd be
if you hadn't gotten scared
and run off

back to your pillow
and its wonderful comfortable
smothering
embrace.

The Reach and the Grasp

Laying here in bed tonight
while my son
sleeps,
the day's work done
and a few minutes left
before sleep hits,

I thought
how good
a cold beer
would taste.

That idea
for me,
is not such a good thing,
though you likely won't understand
unless you been there
yourself.

I have a friend,
a nurse,
who knows.

She's gone years,
but a few weeks ago
thought, too,
how good
a beer would be.

The problem
for each of us,
is that sitting right up next
to the part
with the one beer smile

is the part
that simply wants
to turn off the world
and slip away
into blissful
delicious
oblivion.

And for him,
or her,
or it,
one beer
won't cut it,
nor ten
nor a lifetime.

Knowing and trusting
this realization
usually keeps the reach
just short
of the grasp,

though deeper still
lies the idea
that even with
knowing
the hell that awaits,

sometimes going back out
seems worth it.

And such
a terrifying thought
kept me up
that night
long past
the time
for blissful
sleep.

Hero

Bled out
in the desert
when the truck exploded
taking my arms and legs.

Shipped home
in the dark night,
got buried deep,
under a stone
carved word
HERO.

Don't know about that, though.
Just drove a truck.
Never shot anyone.
Couldn't drink a legal beer.

I'm glad I died,
I don't have to be there anymore;
though I'd always lie and say
if someone were to ask,
I'd go back if I could,
at least until
my friends
get out.

No one asks the dead anything
These days.

I'm not complaining,

or scared

or feeling fucked over.

Its nice here;

I can't get blown up

anymore.

Pretty Words

You know
even with
all these pretty words
about peace
letting go
dharma
and joy

there's a big chunk
of hidden canvas
showing the piles of dusty crap
accumulated everywhere

the algae tank
that maybe still has
a fish or two

a Buick
with no muffler

nights without end
hiding in books
or surfing

so much coffee
it makes
me sick

antidepressants
cigarettes
and potato chips

crowding out
hiding
dying

little by little

Everything

There's no such thing
as a spiritual disease,
nothing to heal,
nothing lost,
nothing to get.

The stuff that happened
when you were a kid
wasn't your fault;
you weren't a lying cheating
selfish child,
not at heart.

So, whatever clouded
the pure truth you already knew,
well, think about it for a second:
what else could you have done?

There's good reasons
why you can't sleep;
they might need exploring,
so put down your cigarette
and the big blue tome,
and take a moment or two
just with self.

Even if
such a thing
as god
really really exists,
the personal happiness
of your ego
can't possibly be
on its to-do list,

which means
no divine plan
with you
in a starring role.

And by the way,
did I say
just because
you feel bad
and think
you're a broken toy,
doesn't make it so?

Maybe
you shouldn't
always
believe
everything you think.

Not being the center
of the universe
isn't a bad thing,
you'll get used to it.

Merely trying
to live life
so that what you do
doesn't make it harder
for anyone else
to live their life
may just be
the most spiritually sublime
act of an awakened being.

A quiet mind
is indeed possible

Meaning,
purpose,
truth,
love,
and wisdom
already rest within,

so when you learn
to turn over and let go
and thereby
grind down
those unfortunate habits
of mind,

you might just find
everything
you ever looked for
all those years
gone by.

It Finds You

I used to ride around
in George Gonder's mustang fastback,
while he rammed his way up and down the gears
and we searched endlessly for something to do.

It was 1973
and neither of us
could stand it
in that crappy little town,

although the cherry vodka and pot
helped a little.

He'd come by around dark,
and off we'd go,
riding Missouri Boulevard
up towards downtown,
around the west side
and back,
until midnight hit
and I had to go home.

George bought it one night
out on the highway
south of town.

We got word
pretty much instantly.
That's how news passes
when you're in high school.

All the girls cried.

George would have liked that,
since they didn't ever seem
to give him much thought
when he was alive.

From then on,
I had my own car,
got a girlfriend,
eventually moved away.

It took another twenty five years
before realizing
you don't have to search
for something to do.

Tall Cows

We lived in a farm house
on a Brown Swiss dairy.

Those cows
were as tall as me.

Pigs too
and my dog
took a chicken just for fun
every few days
when no one
was looking.

We stole mattresses
from where I lived before
and smoked pot every night
under summer clouds.

But it wasn't heaven
not with all the fighting
and how the other folks there
took it

when I got my own place
two months later

like somehow
its not allowed
the moving on business.

Me and Mary
we figured out
we were hostages
and brought our stolen mattress with us
when we left.

That was a bad thing
apparently
because the next night
all hell broke loose

and it wasn't until
I mentioned their marijuana garden
out by the well
that stuff finally
settled down.

They sure were tall cows
though.

Pendulum

People like me
we worry way too much
about how we're feeling
and what we're thinking
and whether stuff's going
the way it should.

And when there's pain
we ride this pendulum
between thinking
how fucking rotten
all those other people are
to how fucking rotten
 we are,

all the while never noticing
that maybe being obsessed
with such foolishness

might not
be the
best use
of these
fleeting
days.

one last time

i haven't cried in years
not since my boy
got sick
and i really learned
how tough
you got to be
sometimes
just to barely get by

its been even longer
since there's been the kind of love
where you can't get someone out of your head
and every inch of her skin
makes for fire in your belly

there's laughter
that's for sure
but not like
when you're young
and stuff's
piss your pants funny

now these years
circle around
faster each time
so that you don't even remember
what it was like
when a day was a long time

but there's always the hope

for something intense enough

to make you sit up

and take notice

and care enough

to feel

without

reservation

one

last

time

Open Heart

I

It was the rum that saved me
from imploding
in utter despair
at the horror my life
became.

Such an end
happens to anyone
abiding in a failed universe,
whose dreams die
and hopes slither off
into whichever crack is closest,
leaving whatever they'd become
out to rust
in icy rain.

If you stay drunk enough though,
none of that matters.

II

Liquid nirvana,
Roshi calls it,
Enlightenment in a bottle,
medicine
for impossibly
wounded
hearts.

So, in all candor
it was the best choice
this small mind found
at the time.

Eventually
the rum
quit working,
goddammit,
and no matter
how much drunk
I got
remained
still thirsty.

Only now
there were shakes,
puking,
bleary gooey
nervous belly,
staggering falling
bruised up mess
of everyday life
to go along

with my pathetic
pretending
how everything
was
just
fine.

All of which in turn,

became

another

glorious

reason

to drink,

until finally

everything

touched

turns to shit,

and though still awake enough

maybe

to put gas in the car

or wash a t shirt

from time to time,

nothing matters,

because

truth be told

you already

fucking may as well

be dead.

III

Eventually

I put down the bottles

and left the bars,

which seems
a stupid thing
unless you been there
yourself,

then you know,
way beyond words
lord how you know,
its not stupid
at all,
but gritty hard work.

That much
my alcoholic brain
saw all along;
it was
another reason
to drink,

because for years
it seemed
there just wasn't
enough me
for such
a difficult
endeavor
as grown up life.

IV

The truly long run hard part here,
though, isn't any of that,

but later
when the cool cool joy
of waking up sober day after day,
hanging out
with all your
way neato new
best friends,
and noticing again
after so many years
the cool white light of a full moon,

begins to fade.

And all the rancid crap
you tried drowning,
way back when
comes in off the bench
all rested and pissed-off
ready to raise hell
again.

V

That's where the rubber
meets the road,

when every twitch,
every habit,
every fiber of being
conspires,
to put drinking me
back in the cockpit

for another go
down the gauntlet
to sweet
liquid
oblivion.

Of cops,
and piss,
and puke,
and nasty bad
bar room jukes;

of hard feelings
and utter desolation,
sick twisted yearning,
and the hatred of children
left to gather
the pieces of their own
broken dreams
long after you're dead
and gone.

Of ruptured arteries,
drowning in your own blood,
and wet brain,
where even the *idea*
of getting sober
loses traction and
slides right into the ditch
leaving no trace,
not even a slime trail,

where those few times
when the doctors or the judges
or the wives
make you stop
for awhile
yields shear
unimaginable
shit your pants
terror.

And mostly where
whatever other choices
you think you got
besides being back out
don't look like hope at all,
just brainwashed,
mindless,
zombie hell
that won't work anyway.

VI

This is where
you learn
if the thing
you think you are
really gets it
or not.

This,
right here
right now,
on the cliff
looking down,

where you discover
if its really want bad enough
whatever lesson,
truth, or redemption
there is
for someone
the likes of you.

And its when
this whole new
sober deal
first gets
really
really
hard.

VII

I have finally
begun to learn
my dharma
is only true
for me.

And these words -
these thoughts -
even they
just don't quite
come together right,

but simply
at best
maybe reach
a sort of approximation
of what it is
that makes even
the least bit of sense
probably just for me.

So when I speak
of open hearts
and letting go,

there's just no telling
what you'll hear
and think

nor any reason
to try and make
what makes sense
to me
do so, too,
for you.

VIII

There's a series
of somehow
loud clicks
you can almost hear
down deep
in tired worn bones,
when stuff dawns
in otherwise stubborn
rigid brains,

where it seems
like something
really new,
and true,
and fucking obvious
hits at depth,
changing
everything.

The first for me
came with the realization
that no matter what
and no matter who
and no matter when
and no matter how bad
it gets,

I just
can't drink.

The day
when that choice worked
is long gone,
ain't never
ever coming back.

IX

Then there came,
a little later,
the realization
that them not quite drowned
demons weren't so real
as to stand
beyond reproach

weren't too loud
to scare the wind

weren't too brash
to run the show,

and weren't so strong
that they'd really
do me in.

After all,
whatever thoughts
my brain oozes
are just ideas
worn bare,
perceptions
imperfectly cast,
colored lenses
turned to habit
and dug to ruts

so long ago
they speak
the voice of fathers
to ears
of a children

and vice versa.

X

And the third notion,
still coming,
like everything else,

is simply how the mind's puke
isn't true or real enough
to require
ultimate submission
nor conquering.

I am not
my brain's bitch,
nor its daddy.

Neither running from
nor to,
these things thought
become just another color to see,
or sound to hear,
or smell and taste to appreciate,
before the next moment hits
and your day moves on.

XI

And in it all,
its as if
there's layers
to this thing called self,

so that
whittling and grinding,
first about drink,
and then, perhaps, fear
or loss, or pain,

I reach the place
whereupon once
was hoped
to be a pure whole me,

only to find
more wood and stone
to sculpt away.

And where then
in time
comes the clarity,
felt deep deep down,

how all those alleged truths
were far less
stone floor
and far more,
steel bars,

sealed and locked
way beyond when
the prisoners
earned parole.

XII

All we ever do
is walk this path,
from when they pull us
out our mothers' bellies,
and not finished yet.

No end in sight,

no rest,

no turning back.

No arriving

no departing

no beginning

no completion.

Just breathing

and doing

and thinking

and feeling,

No more

and likewise

never

any less.

That's what they are,

these lives

we live,

whether sober,

drunk,

awake,

or asleep,

deluded by warm fuzzy blankets,

the babbling rhetoric of scripture,

the sexy smart rich lure of tomorrow's next best thing,

or wakened
to the Truth,
beyond words,
our hearts
know best.

How could
it be
any different?

XIII

I've done my life many ways,
usually with
the conscious thought
that whichever this
was it
could finally lay
some sort
of lasting peace
upon a sad soul.

And in that time,
never once saw
such notions
as anything other
than obvious,
anything other than
what you do,
anything other
than who I was.

But letting rest
that fool's errand
snipe hunt
for some missing ingredient,

the lid opens
on far more
than even Roshis
know.

XIV

Because,
if I am not
a weak small child
than I need not
defend that boy.

If I need not
defend that boy,
than I may set
my armor down.

And in that place
where walls and moats
once stretched across these fields,

tress and grasses
grow again
beneath the shining moon.

Run for Cigarettes

We made a run
for cigarettes
right before bed
together
the other night

and all I could think
was how
for so long
I believed
the days
where there was someone
beautiful and loving
and light and open
like her
for me

were so far gone
I can't even remember

Last Zazen

Its one thing
to think
how life and death
aren't two,

and another to taste it
first hand.

My friend died last night,
out of the blue in mid step.

When we found out,
right before morning zazen,
it seemed there ought to be
something to do
besides simply doing
what we always did.

In the end though,
we lit the candle,
bowed,
and rang the bell
just like always.

After it was over,
I turned to tidy the alter,
and saw his cushion
flat and flipped the wrong way
also, just like always,

and thought how
for so long
we always straightened
and fixed his space for him,
before bowing out.

This would be
the last time
for that.

Somehow both
numb and sad
we put his rakasu
down at the cushion
and moved,
all frozenlike,
into the morning sun.

Life and death
aren't two.

Neither is sitting
and mourning,
remembering
and forgetting,
holding
and letting
go.

The stone steps
he nearly finished
felt rock solid
under my feet,

though they too
will someday crumble
when the time comes.

Photographs

By the time the trial ended
I didn't know
whether the crime
was the threat
she said he made,

or merely the scary homeless
ranting fear
he stood for.

I suppose though the lady was right,
how when he reached in his pocket
it *might* have been a gun or knife or something,

but fact was
he pulled out a camera,
not a weapon,

that he used
to help remember
the angry people
worth staying away from
no matter what.

She'd earned
that designation
by calling the cops
and saying he threatened
to hurt her.

Any fool could see
this was bullshit,

except the prosecutor.

Which made for two
smug pissed off people
trying to show
how dangerous and crazy
he was.

In the end none of it mattered.
Its the jury that calls the balls and strikes
and they sent him home
an innocent man
after about ten minutes,

though no one felt too good
about any of it.

It just proves
how stupid juries are,
the prosecutor concluded;

there's a knife in a pocket
with her name on it,
the woman still believes;

and my guy will always know
there's folks out to get him
just for being
what he can't help.

Literal Nirvana

I wonder
if the feeling a man gets
right at the point
of penetration

is as good
as the feeling a woman seems to get
when he sticks it in her?

There's a glazed look
that washes across
her face when she's taken

that seems
literally,
like nirvana,

as her eyes
fog over
and her lips part
when she swallows
the moment

before arching up
and melting into
the pillows and blankets
in sweaty passionate sticky communion.

It gets me hard
just thinking about it.

Make Me Smile

These bright green trees
slipping through
morning fog
below a thin band
of clear sky
and the mass of gray seething clouds
looming everywhere else
make me smile

This Now

Here's the scary part
what you thought
the core
turns out's
just dust
layered
in a certain way
though it might
have been
easily
otherwise

And all the while
never noticed
life and death
mark time
in this now
that never ends

Shimmering Dharma Moon

They don't like these Zen poems
near as much
as the ones
about sex or drinking.

I get lots of kudos for them,
but these here
where open hearts and mist
is about all that happens
just don't seem
to get people's attention.

I should try a car chase
through fields of pompous grass
under a shimmering dharma moon

It'd never end.

Russet Potatoes

The shaking
gets so bad
that though there's dreams

of fast as lightening running,
back to the man,
the store,
wherever

to drink or smoke
or sniff or shoot
whatever
someone says
gets you off
like a motherfucker

truth is
you can't hardly walk,
don't give a shit,
piss your pants,
sleep in puke,
pale sunless skin,
and blistered wounds
where hair used to grow,

wonder
at who the fuck's
up in the attic whispering
all night long,

till they come with a big bag
and haul you away
like so many pounds
of Russet potatoes.

It gets worse,
even then
and even when
that seems
impossible,

'til the world
shrinks down
to your head and belly,
and everything else
is sorta like
watching
bad bad TV
from the big end
of a funnel

where all you want
is a smoke
or sleep

and a way to turn off
the fucking noise.

Liquid Asphalt

The road dips and curves
through pine groves and walnut forests,
before popping out
along the ridgeline
then descending down again
to some unnamed stream,
over and over
for 45 miles.

I knew it better than most men know their wives.
Drove it both ways daily
for 4 years,
in light and dark,
through thunder storms and blizzards,
and the hot Missouri Summer,
when the asphalt turns liquid by noon.

There was an old town you'd go through,
where though they once had a couple of stores,
now all it was
was a gas station
and an outside pop machine.

I'd stop there at night for something with caffeine,
and once a shot of whiskey
with three guys standing there in the dark
who said if I didn't drink they'd beat my ass.

There were old farms along the way,
and a couple of them churches
with no minister
so they just come in on Sundays
and sing and read aloud
together from the bible
for an hour or two.

I'd blow buy
in a cloud of hot sticky yellow dust,
sometimes hearing the music
though that may have just been
my imagination.

There was a girlfriend then
whom I was luckier to have
then vice versa;
she'd wait up for me
at night
and fuck my brains out
before I even got into the shower.

Did it for herself
as much as me,
which was a first
since I was only 23
and had only known the ones
with obligations.

We'd stay up late smoking pot
or go out for music and beer and friends
night after night.

She didn't know the road like me, though,
and just thought
it was a long commute.

Everything's always more
than what it seems.
Usually we just don't notice.
But with the road
I didn't have that problem.

I wish it was around now
to drive.

Childish Dreams

You can talk about letting go of stuff all you want,
but late at night when most people gratefully snooze away
while you still laying there hurting,
don't be surprised when what comes flooding back
are all the wishes and wants and desires once lived by
and still secretly hoped for
there in the bed
with the blinds drawn.

Having someone to love
who loves you back
more or less even-steven,

living a nice enough life
where there's a little fun
and not too much struggle
just to get by,

and the car runs and the bills get paid
and you're not collapsing into the sack every night
having run out of time
with stuff still to do,
day after day,

and where what goes on in your brain
isn't as loud and demanding
as the sound of life outside,
so that this moment
right here and now
gets its full due attention.

Letting go
isn't so easy,
and if you're honest enough
to admit it,
sometimes there's no mere getting over
what was lost or never had,

as you lay there thinking
how it sure would be nice
for something sweet and easy
to come wandering
down the path,

to hold your hand
in the next leg
of the journey home

The Only Universe I have Ever Known

I believe beliefs are overrated.

I believe what I think
isn't a very good representation
of anything
but what I think.

I think after awhile all these
concepts and assumptions and ideas
become pretty good walls
but not so good doors.

I believe there isn't really a me
that resembles anything
remotely like
the little boy
or the grown man
he became.

I believe the boundary
between where my life ends
and yours begins
is an illusion.

And I believe even that belief
is wrong
or at least
incomplete.

I believe the sound of the bell,
the lure of the bottle,
and the sweat of hard labor
are all a piece
of the very same cake.

I believe the seamless tapestry
of this mind life,
whether embraced eagerly like a child,
or warily
like a wild hungry bear,
cares little
for the neurotic worry
of ego's past errors,

and goes merrily on
inexorably towards a fitting end,
naked and alone.

I sometimes wonder
when that time comes
if there'll be
begging and crying
for the alluring embrace
of long dead
mommies and daddies,
in gut level remorse
for a life
lived poorly,

or maybe standing up
in this place now
brave and aware,
neither glancing
forward nor back,

as these billowing waves of mind
bring a seamless end
to the only universe
I have ever known.

I turned fifty this year. When I was a little kid, I wondered what that would be like. It was a foolish endeavor, chock full of dreamlike fantasies of rock stardom or being an important person. This was the early seventies. I lived on the trailing cusp of the baby boom where a pervasive sense of futility prevailed, as the childlike optimism of the former decade gave way to meaningless drug use and escape for its own sake.

In Buddhism there is talk of the Realm of Hungry Ghosts, a world populated by beings whose insatiable desires are thwarted by an inability to satisfy their cravings. It is not a happy place, as many in my generation can attest. No quantity of drugs, sex, stuff, therapy, career, or religious escape quenches our thirst.

I tried, though. I was a pot head, a social worker, an alcoholism counselor, a biker, a lawyer, a musician, an Episcopalian, a philosopher, a political candidate, a carny, a campaign staffer, an alcoholic, a pancake cook, and a husband (twice) and a father (once). I've lived in 14 towns in seven States, with five different women. Each chapter had its moments, but like any bad novel, the end never satisfies whatever hopes you held when the book was opened.

My teacher's teacher, Katagiri Roshi, used to talk about being in a corner where you can't move an inch. He spoke of how in that moment there arises – perhaps for the first time ever – a true opportunity to experience real silence. And, in that place, where its just you and your demons, there is a real chance for real change.

On the Fourth of July, 2004, I found myself in that corner. I had a moment of clarity, and the beginnings of a psychic change.

I started writing poetry in the Fall of 2005. The words have poured out in huge chunks, with no end in sight, leading to my first book, This Now, and these twin collections, Always Doing Being We Live Our Lives, and The Only Universe I Have Ever Known. Together they comprise a memoir of sorts, a running commentary on these last fifty years. I didn't get to be a rock star; I'm not an important person. I don't even remember all that much about what it was like being that kid way back when, wondering what the future held.

But I do know about the realm of Hungry Ghosts. I understand what it means to always need to change how I feel. I'm able to see the outlines of the corner where you can't move an inch. And for whatever reason, I find myself writing poems about it all.

Taiyu John Robertson
October, 2007

For David, Shoken, the Sangha, and everyone who has shared even a small piece of their recovery with me.

Impermanence is swift; practice with diligence.